Praise for *Rent to Own*

"This is an excellent book! It teaches you a practical, proven method of investing and becoming financially successful from the ground up."

— **Brian Tracy,** speaker, author, and consultant, author of *The Psychology of Achievement* and *Eat That Frog!*

"*Rent to Own Real Estate: From Factory to Financial Freedom* offers a unique and highly profitable method of generating income. Jerry's book provides clear, easy to understand instructions for making money with real estate that most beginners know little about. Tested and proven, this specialized technique allowed the author to kiss his factory job goodbye.

This book provides a step-by-step plan for beginners and ol' salts alike. Rent to own works well in almost every market or location because the rental housing supply is always less than demand. The number one principle of any successful venture is; *find a need and fill it.* Jerry's book shows you how to accomplish that and profit very well from doing it."

— **"Fixer Jay" Jay P. DeCima,** the king of fixer-uppers, a seasoned real estate investor and author of *Investing In Fixer-Uppers*

"After being a real estate investor and teacher for over four decades every once in a while, someone like Jerry comes along who graduates from student to teacher. This book is very important for anyone to read that's thinking about getting into real estate and makes the case that anyone can do it. Jerry is a great example of going from a job slave to a multi millionaire by simply applying techniques that have worked for decades, but won't be discovered unless one puts in an effort to learn the ropes. It's obvious in this book that Jerry has learned the ropes and reaped the rewards and has a deep seated interest in helping others to do the same. I read the entire book in one sitting because I simply couldn't put it down. Jerry's story reminds me a lot about my story and it took one seminar for me to change my direction for the rest of my life and affect thousands of others. Perhaps this book could be your turning point. It's based in reality and it's pretty obvious the author practices what he preaches."

— **Ron LeGrand,** nationally renowned real estate expert, "The Guru" of quick turn real estate, author of *How To Be A Quick Turn Real Estate Millionaire*

"Jerry Hines should have written this book 10 years ago! Anyone that reads this book and acts in implementing the principles, will be successful investing in real estate. I know this, because I have implemented the principles. I have learned from Jerry and have made money investing in real estate. After reading *Rent to Own Real Estate: From Factory to Financial Freedom*, I now have so many more ideas and strategies to implement in my real estate business."

— **Bradley Horner,** CEO of BSH Enterprises

"It's been fun and encouraging to watch Jerry progress in the local real estate market. I am grateful to have helped be a part of his journey. If you know Jerry you know positivity radiates from his inner core. It has been great to see him transition from the steel mill to running his own real estate business. Jerry always has a positive outlook on life. You can definitely tell he has a 'burning desire' for real estate, his family and most importantly God."

— **Michael Stark,** President/CEO of Carrollton Federal Bank

RENT TO OWN
REAL E$TATE

RENT TO OWN REAL E$TATE
FROM FACTORY TO FINANCIAL FREEDOM

JERRY HINES

ISBN 979-8-9919019-0-1 (paperback)
ISBN 979-8-9919019-1-8 (ebook)

Cover and interior design by Jenneth Leed, jennethleed.com

I dedicate this book to John Higgins.

You were my teacher, friend, encourager and real estate mentor. You were always willing to listen and encourage. You dedicated your life to helping others achieve.

I won't forget!

Table of Contents

Introduction

There are a hundred books that tell you how to buy, fix and sell houses. The television shows call this flipping a house. I'm not going to explain that process in detail even though that is how I got my start. This book will instruct you on one way to make money when the economy tanks and houses are not selling. This book explains one way to make money with real estate using the rent-to-own (RTO) philosophy. Notice I said **one way**. There are a thousand different ways to do it. I have found a way to make money and have fun at the same time. If you don't have fun investing in real estate, then go do something else with your life. Life is too short to be miserable while you're making money.

1

My Factory Story and The Magic Moment

There are moments in life when you know that if a certain thing had not happened or if a certain person had not been there for you, your life would have been totally different. Well, the following story describes just such a moment.

I had been working in factories for 20 years. I started as a lab tech in the chemical manufacturing industry. I worked there for $2^{1/2}$ years when 35 of us were called for a meeting in the lunchroom. We were told we were going to be permanently laid off.

I quickly found another job as a chemist with a chemical recycling company. Six months later a new company bought them out. It was a smooth transition and almost all of the employees at the factory kept their jobs. This was a good company. I had the opportunity to try several different jobs here. I finally landed in the position of Safety Manager. I was there for 13 years when again, we were bought out. This was a hostile takeover. It wasn't pretty and several hundred people lost their jobs. Eighteen months later this new company declared Chapter 11 bankruptcy. More people were terminated. After that, we went through a series of reorganizations. Each year, usually the week before Christmas, several hundred people were told they were no longer needed under the latest organizational restructure. It was after the second reorganization that I could see into the future. My number was going to come up; I just didn't know when.

In 2004 I read a book by Dan Miller titled *48 Days To The Work You Love*. No, I didn't find the work I now love 48 days after reading this book, but what I did learn was to put my goals, dreams and visions in **written** form. This was a monumental discovery for me. After putting my goals into writing, I began looking into business opportunities that would get me out of the factory setting. I researched several different business models and then I went to a seminar in 2005 where several motivational speakers were delivering their messages. One of the speakers was very entertaining and he spoke about his successes at buying, fixing and selling houses. I liked what I heard. In early 2006 I went to a one day seminar on real estate investing. It cost $100 and I could take my wife, Susan, for free. She sat through the entire seminar with me, and she even took notes. At the end of that day, I was fired up! I wanted to buy something and give it a try. As we drove home, she listened to my excitement. When I finally calmed down and took a breath, she gently reminded me how NOT-handy I was. Ouch! That hurt. She was right. I could change a light bulb and plunge a toilet but that was about the limit of my home repair abilities. Now what?

I had what Napoleon Hill would call "A Burning Desire." I really wanted out of the factory in the worst way. One evening, as Susan and I sat on the couch discussing my dream of buying investment real estate, I had a brilliant idea. I knew that my father-in-law, Don, could fix anything. In fact, for the previous 30 years he had made his living as a handyman/cabinet maker in South Florida. So...I asked her, "If I can get your dad to agree to help me fix a house, can I buy it?" She immediately said, "Yes. If you can get my dad up here to help you finish the house, you can buy it." I repeated the question, because I wanted to make sure my wife understood what she had just agreed to. I was serious. "Yes," was her answer back. I immediately picked up the phone and called South Florida. I told Don the whole story. I told him I would supply all the money. I needed his knowledge, experience, and time. He immediately said yes! He said he had always wanted to flip a house, but he never had the cash to try it. I told him that whatever profit I made on the house, half was his. If I made one dollar, fifty cents was his. If I made $20,000, $10,000 was his. I asked him to tell Susan exactly what he had just told me and I handed her the phone. Two minutes later she hung up the phone, looked at me with a big smile and said, "Go buy a house!" I was excited and scared at the same time.

I went ahead with my dream and my wife reluctantly supported me. We didn't have cash but we did have equity in our home. We went to the bank that held our first mortgage and applied for a home equity line of credit. We were granted a line of credit and I immediately began looking for ugly houses.

I found one! It was a small house, 2 bedrooms,

1 bath. It was in a decent location and in my price range. After I did all the math, I sat down with Susan and told her my plan. I wasn't sure how to make this work, but I wanted to try. A couple of days later I submitted an offer on the house. I bought it. Don drove up and we went to work. I still had my full-time factory job but every day after work and on weekends I was there. We worked every spare moment for over three months. The house was finally finished. I listed it with a realtor in December 2006. Three days after I signed the listing agreement, I had a signed contract to sell it. The house sold in early 2007. After the closing, I calculated all my expenses and I sent Don a check for $10,000. We had made $20,000 on that little house. When Don received the check, he called and told me to go buy another house! He was ready to do it again! That was the beginning of my real estate investing career.

During all the excitement of finishing the house and one week before Christmas in 2006, I was called to the Plant Manager's office and was told that my job had been eliminated in this year's reorganization. My feelings were hurt, but it's not like I didn't see it coming. I cleaned out my desk and said goodbye to a few of the coworkers I had come to greatly respect. I had worked there for 20 years. As I sat in my car in the parking lot, I decided to change my attitude from one of despair to one of thanksgiving. I am a Christian and I have been telling my four children since birth that God watches over us and that no situation is too big for Him to handle. I knew this event in my life did not surprise God. So, was I going to feel sorry for myself, or was I going to look forward to the next adventure that God had prepared for me? My children, ages 20, 17, 13 and 11, would be watching to see if I believed what I said I did. I decided to face this new adventure with God and with a smile.

I got home a little early that day. All my children were home from school because it was the week before Christmas. As usual I got hugs from everyone when I came in. Everyone was happy and smiling. Then, Susan asked me why I was home so early. I hesitated for just a moment. I hadn't prepared a speech for how to tell my family that I no longer had a job. I was about to speak when my 17 year old daughter, Sarah, who is very perceptive about human emotions, blurted out, "Did you quit your job today?" I laughed. I looked over at Susan. Her eyes were wide and her mouth had dropped open. I told Sarah, "Your mother and I need to talk privately." After about ten minutes, Susan and I emerged from our quiet spot and I called a family meeting. I discussed the details. I told them that as long as God gave me breath, we would not lose the house and they would not go hungry. Nothing would change. They had nothing to worry about. There was a brief pause in the conversation then Sarah asked, "Since you don't have a job anymore, does that mean we can go to Florida for Christmas this year?" .... That was the moment I knew that my children were not worried one bit.

During the winter and spring of 2007 I was receiving severance money, 20 weeks of full pay (1 week of pay for every year of service at that location). I was also receiving unemployment. I bought and was working on 2 more houses in that time period. The severance pay and the unemployment were both going to run out in early summer. I wasn't finished with the houses I had purchased, and I was running out of money. The banks would not loan me money because I did not have a J-O-B. I was between a rock and a hard place. I had to go find another job.

The Lord continued to take care of me. Three weeks before my unemployment would run out, a contractor friend called me and asked if I was looking for a job. "As a matter of fact," I told him, "I am." He hand delivered my resume to the Safety Manager at a local steel mill. One week after the unemployment ran out, I had a new job. My intention was to keep the factory job until the income from my real estate investments was paying me the same amount that I was receiving from the steel mill. I continued to work in the steel manufacturing industry until May of 2016. That is when I turned in my resignation. What a glorious moment that was!

At first it was scary. The money that magically appeared in my checking account every two weeks would quit coming. I also would not have enough money to purchase medical insurance. So we prayed and God faithfully took care of us.

There are so many magic moments in life. So many decisions that will change your life's trajectory. The moment in time that has most changed my life was when Don Dunkerley said, "YES!" Without his help and encouragement, I would still be a slave at the factory.

Thanks Don!

2

Prepare Yourself Financially

Before you jump into real estate, I challenge you to change the way you think about money. If you have poor money management habits while making $5,000 a month, you will have poor money management habits when you are making $25,000 a month. The only problem is, you will dig your hole deeper into debt, five times deeper and five times faster. Money is a tool, not a toy. You need to learn how to use the tool to make more money. If you use money simply to make yourself feel better in that moment, you will always be a slave to the dollar bill. I don't know about you, but I want the dollar bills slaving for me, not the other way around.

Years before I started buying real estate, my wife began listening to Dave Ramsey, a nationally known financial advisor, radio talk show host and author. I first started listening to his radio show in the 1990s. At this point in time, I believed I would always have a house payment and a car payment. And by always, I mean until the day I died. That was my reality. Listening to Dave Ramsey changed the way I think. I'm a hard head, so it took me a couple of years of listening to him to take hold of what Dave was trying to get me to understand. What I finally heard was, it is possible and desirable to get out of debt. I wanted to be one of those people who were screaming on his radio show, "I'M DEBT FREE!"

I started reading his books, listening to his radio shows and following his plan. My wife was totally on board. It wasn't long before we were quoting Dave Ramsey in our dinner table conversations. What I didn't realize at the time is that not only did Dave Ramsey change my life, but he also changed the lives of my four children who are all adults now and are way smarter with their money than I was at their age.

Here's the plan. You don't want any debt! Pay off your car, boat, motorcycle, furniture, lawn equipment and all credit cards. Pay everything off except the house you live in and if you can, pay that off too. If you aren't going to pay something off, sell it! If you are sloppy with money going into the real estate business, you will be sloppy with the money you make in your business. You will simply be digging a hole deeper into debt. Work Dave Ramsey's plan.

> **Step #1:** Create an emergency fund of $1,000 and set up a budget. Give every dollar a job.
> **Step #2:** Pay off all debt with the exception of your home. Cut up your credit cards.
> **Step #3:** Build a saving account containing three to six months of normal household expenses in preparation for the major storms of life that will inevitably come.
> **Step #4:** Use 15% of your income to invest for the long term, in mutual funds.

At step four, I chose a different path. I chose to invest in real estate because I can touch it, I understand it, and I like it. Once you buy into Dave Ramsey's baby steps 1, 2 and 3, the sky is the limit for you. You now have control of your money. At the end of those 3 baby steps, each dollar you make will have a job and you will soon have money working for you. What an incredible change in how we think. Stop working for money and have your money work for you.

I encourage you with my "Dave Ramsey" story, because I did not begin buying investment property until after I had control of the money I was bringing home from the factory. That would be my recommendation for you. Cut up your credit cards. Pay off everything except your home then start buying real estate. Take control of your financial future now.

If you jump ahead with me a few years into the future, early in my real estate investing career, I sold one of my houses and made enough money from the sale to pay off the mortgage on my primary residence (I call that my wife's house). At that point we were completely debt free. I called my parents, my brothers and my grown children and asked them to come over for a mortgage burning party. It was a good time and it made a lasting impression on all my family members. They saw it was possible to live without a mortgage payment. A few years after that party, I had saved up enough money to buy the 86 acres behind me with cash (I call that my back yard / gift to me). It's a place for me to hunt, hike and ride my ATV. Dave's plan works. Take control of the income you have today and the income you have tomorrow will be well behaved.

3

Making Offers

Make lots of offers. Most of your offers will be rejected. That's okay. You simply shake the dust off your sandals and go on to the next house. In 2023 I purchased a 3 bedroom 2 bath home with a detached two car garage for $11,700. This stuff is real. You can do this. You just have to keep looking and keep making offers. Practice making offers with this mindset; If you're not embarrassed to make the offer, you're probably paying too much!

After you hear what they want then you get to decide what it's worth to you. Sometimes it surprises me how badly someone wants to get rid of a property. About four years ago I bought a 3 bedroom 1 bath brick home on 0.6 acres in a rural setting for $5,000. It had a serious foundation problem but for $5,000 I was willing to give it a shot.

A few years ago, I was walking through a house in Pleasureville, KY, that was listed with a realtor. The lady who lived there had died and the heirs were selling the house. After my walk through, I had my realtor write up the offer. It was about 30% less than the asking price. I had my realtor add on to the offer that the washer, dryer, stove, refrigerator, upright freezer and microwave were to be left as a condition of the sale. Three hours after the offer was sent to the sellers, it was returned to my realtor marked "Accepted." My realtor called me and told me she had never seen anything like that before. I told her to get use to it. She was going to see stranger things than that if she continued working with me.

When looking for a realtor, find one that is willing to make your offer and present it with a straight face. Imagine your realtor showing up to the seller's agents office with eyes downcast and an embarrassed smile. How would you receive that offer? You want someone who will walk in boldly, and present any offer you send. It may take some time to find a realtor with this much self-confidence, but it's worth the search.

4

Your First Purchase

I have had many people come to me over the past 15 years asking me how to get started. I tell them all the same thing. Just buy one. Just start with one house and see if you like it. It really is hard to lose money buying houses when you buy the right one for the right price. Find a decent neighborhood and try to buy the ugliest house in that neighborhood. For your first house, I would advise you to stay away from the manufactured homes, i.e. single wide mobile homes and double wide mobile homes. Manufactured homes require more maintenance. Start with a stick built house. Negotiate a good deal, then when you are handed the keys, begin making the house pretty.

A good book for you to read is Napoleon Hill's *Think and Grow Rich*. In this book, Mr. Hill goes into great detail about having a "Burning Desire!" He advises that you use that burning desire to motivate you into action. It's easy to read a hundred books on how to buy and profit from real estate investments. But buying your first one will scare the chocolate out of you. It's scary when it's your money, your credit, your signature, and your responsibility. If you make money, you did it. If you lose money, you did it. The first property is the hardest. After 10 it gets easy. After 20 it becomes fun. After 30, you find yourself training attorneys and realtors on what can and cannot be done. It's a hoot to sit in a closing and have a young mortgage broker, banker, title agent or realtor tell you something is impossible or illegal and can't be done when you know it is not illegal and you have already done 3 deals just like that this year. It's fun to watch your grown children doing real estate deals larger than anything you ever thought possible. This feels good.

If you dread going to work every day, you need to change the way you think. What is your burning desire?

5

The Difference Between Flip and Rent-To-Own

When you flip a property, you repair or replace everything that needs it, and make everything beautiful. The retail buyer coming into this house wants a house that looks and smells brand new. There are hundreds of books on how to fix and flip homes.

In an RTO home you make sure everything works, but you don't make everything like new. In general, the tenant buyer will take better care of the home than a renter but they will not maintain or repair anything.

Do's and Don'ts in an RTO home:

- Do clean the house top to bottom and kill all bugs.

- Do clean out the gutters and make sure the roof does not leak.

- Do manicure the lawn, trim the bushes and trees, pick up all trash. Make the yard look good. The neighbors will love you.

- Do fix all holes in the walls.

- Do make sure all doors open and close properly.

- Do paint everything white. It makes the house look larger and cleaner.

- Do fix trip hazards and anything unsafe.

- Do make sure all lights, outlets and electrical systems work properly.

- Do clean light fixtures and replace low watt light bulbs with brighter bulbs.

- Don't install storm doors. Tenant buyers have pets and children. These two bundles of energy will tear out the screens in the first month.

- Don't install screens into windows. Same reason as above.

- Don't replace the carpet or vinyl unless it is a trip hazard. Tenant buyers will destroy it within 12 months anyway. Clean the carpet, but don't replace it.

- Don't replace counter tops. They will use the counter top as a cutting board during the first month.

- Don't install new central heat and air if it is not already there. The tenant buyer will never change the filter. If baseboard heaters and window AC units are what were there when you bought the house then make sure they work and leave them.

- Don't replace light fixtures unless they are broken.

- Don't replace the roof unless it leaks or is in bad shape. If it looks like it will make it another 5 years, leave it alone.

- Don't install window treatments of any kind. Let the tenant buyer do their own thing.

6

From Flipping To RTOs and Why

I began my real estate investing career in 2006 by doing what the television shows now call "flipping." I bought a house, made it beautiful and sold it. I bought two in 2007 and sold them. I bought 3 in 2008 and I bought 3 more in 2009. In the fall of 2008 the economy was in a downward spiral. By 2009 it became hard to give houses away. I had 3 rehab houses in process at that time and I was running out of money. Nothing was selling. I had to come up with another exit strategy. The buy, fix and sell model was not working. I knew I did not want to be a landlord. I knew I did not want to be someone's mommy and daddy, on call 24/7 to fix every little thing they wanted to whine about. I had read about the rent to own process and I had gone to a week long seminar with Ron Legrand where lease options were taught. I had three choices: hold onto my fix and flip game plan and go bankrupt, become a landlord and start renting my beautiful houses to people who would probably tear them up, or come up with a plan to sell my houses via Rent-To-Own. I chose door number three. I read all about it. I believed I could do it. I had a burning desire to succeed. And I did! I still enjoy the fix and flip model more, but when houses are not selling, the rent-to-own process is the next best thing.

7

Where To Start In The RTO Process

First you need a house. There are hundreds of books on how to find, buy, fix and flip a house. Read five or six of these books then go buy yourself a house. When the market is hot; I find, buy, fix and then sell the house as fast as I can. However, when the market goes cold and it is hard to sell a home, I make passive income selling houses as rent-to own. This book describes in detail how to have fun and make money by selling your houses as rent-to-own.

Okay, you've read the books. You've been watching the market. It is a buyer's market. That's good because today, you are a buyer. You found the house you want. You bought it. You got a good deal. Now, before you jump into this project, you know you are not going to be able to fix and quickly sell this house and make a decent profit because there are a ton of houses on the market and houses just aren't selling. So, when you decide that you are going to do a rent-to-own you are going to FIX this house. You are NOT going to make it beautiful. You will get most of your rent-to own houses back and no one is going to take care of your house the way that you would. So DON'T put fancy stuff in this house.

I always fix the exterior of the house first because I don't want any complaints from the neighbors and I want the city inspection people to see that when Jerry Hines buys a property, he makes all of the ugly disappear. The city officials get no more complaints about the property and they like that.

Where to start? Trim the trees. Pick up all the trash. Remove the giant ugly bushes that cover the front of the house. Don't just trim these big ugly bushes; get rid of them. The new tenant buyers will never trim them and in three years the bushes will look worse than when you bought the house. Mow and use a weed-eater. Get rid of the 50 year old TV antenna and the six satellite dishes. Get rid of the three broken swing sets. Straighten or remove the broken down fence. There are four cable TV wires and two old telephone land line wires running to the house. The sky over the back yard looks like a spider web. Get rid of all these wires. All these wires are attached to the exterior of the house via ugly plastic boxes. Get rid of these boxes. Seems like every house has a pile of rocks in the yard. Get rid of them. Get rid of the concrete goose and the concrete pig. Bleach the exterior of the house if needed. If the roof is in decent shape but it looks stained, bleach the stains and algae off the roof. If the roof looks like it might have 5 years of life left in it, leave it. If it looks like it could begin leaking in 2 or 3 years, you probably ought to replace it now. Clean out the gutters. Bleach the exterior of the gutters and fix them so they hang straight. Paint the exterior of the house if needed. Replace broken windows. Do not put in new windows and never install screens or storm doors. Window screens and storm doors are not strong enough to survive a tenant buyer. Fix the deck and handrail. Make the exterior look so nice that the neighbors will come over to thank you. It happens to me on almost every house. Some of your neighbors will want to look on the inside. They see the transformation that has taken place on the outside. They conclude that if the outside of the house looks good, so does the inside. Do not let these people into your house. The inside is still a wreck. You have not done anything to the inside yet. You spent the first three weeks making the exterior look good so the neighbors would not call the mayor to complain. If you let these people wander around inside your junk house, you will regret it. They will be disappointed because it is still ugly inside. They will waste your time with questions and stories. Some will want you to give them the junk inside the house. Don't do it. Just tell them to check back with you in a couple of months. The house will look much better then. They won't be back. They were just curious about who you are and what you are doing. It's just something new for them to think about.

Let's move to the interior. When necessary, and it frequently is, rent a 40 cubic yard dumpster and clean out the house. If it's not attached to the house and it's not an appliance, throw it out. Clean the light fixtures and put light bulbs with the highest number of lumens in every fixture. Clean the carpet. Do not install new carpet unless areas of the old carpet have become trip hazards. If you put in new carpet, it will just make you mad because the tenant buyers will not take care of it and you will have to replace it again when they leave. Just give what's there a good cleaning. If people have been living there with window AC units and baseboard heat, leave it alone. If it has central heat and air but it does not work, repair it. Don't put a new central HV/AC in this house unless the old one is not repairable. You don't need that expense right now and the house will RTO without it, trust me! If the kitchen cabinets are functional and the countertop is not destroyed, give them a good cleaning and leave them. For a large, damaged spot in a counter top, I have cut the bad spot out and inserted a cutting block to fill the hole. It works great and looks pretty good. Sweep all the walls and ceilings and put a fresh coat or two or three of white primer paint throughout the house. I never use "finish" paint in the houses. Only white primer goes on walls, doors, ceiling and trim. Think of it as giving the buyer a clean, blank canvas to work with. In my experience, they rarely repaint, so it is easy to freshen up the walls with another coat of primer when you get the house back. White paint makes everything look bigger and brighter. You want the house to look clean and bright. Make sure there are no water leaks. Make sure the water heater works.

Make sure all the electrical outlets work. Make sure everything in the house works. If I bought the house with appliances that work, I clean them and leave them with the house. I never buy appliances for an RTO house. If there are no working appliances, the buyer will have to provide their own, and they do.

When you are done fixing and painting the house, clean everything, including the windows and window frames. Make it spotless clean. Mow and weed eat the yard. Now you are ready to make some money.

8

Items To Acquire To Jump Start Your RTO Machine

- Phone system capable of having multiple voice mail boxes
- Copier
- RTO signs (make your own in your garage if you want: I do!)
- Computer with printer and scanner
- White poster board 22" X 28" (Exhibit A – Chapter 14)

- Home Ownership Application (Exhibit B – Chapter 15)

- Applicant Information Sheet (Exhibit C – Chapter 15)

- Lease with an Option to Purchase Agreement (Exhibit D – Chapter 16)

You don't need any of these items today. First you have to find and buy a house. While you are working on the house, getting it ready for your tenant buyer, then you will need to begin pulling the RTO supplies together.

9

Deciding What To Charge For Your RTO

Before we dive into the math, I need to give you some background information so the LOW numbers I use here don't put you into shock.

I live and do my business in rural Kentucky. My entire county has a population estimated at 8,600 people. You probably have more people than that in your neighborhood. I can purchase beat up houses for less than $100,000 even today, 2024. I know that most of you are paying three times that amount and sometimes more for an ugly house. I'm not suggesting everyone move to the hills of Kentucky; I just want you to know that the dollar figures in this book are real. My figures may be low compared to your area, but they are real here in rural Kentucky. The rent-to-own process that I describe in this book will work whether you are selling for $150,000 or $450,000. The process is the same; it's just that the numbers are larger where you live. So let's get started with the numbers that are more common where I live.

Let's say the purchase price was $90,000. After all your fix up costs and holding costs, you have another $15,000 invested. You are into this house for $105,000. The market is a buyers' market so selling it as a flip will not be very profitable.

$90,000	Purchase Price
$15,000	Fix up costs
$105,000	Total invested

First, figure out how much money is coming out of your pocket each month while you own this house. What is the principal and interest payment on a $105,000 bank loan. Let's say the interest rate is 7% fixed for 30 years. Principal and interest is $700/month. For simplicity's sake let's say the taxes are $1,200/year and the insurance is $1,200/year. In this situation the taxes will add $100/month to your ownership costs and insurance will add another $100/month to your ownership costs. $700 + $100 + $100 = $900/month. Now the question you ask yourself is how much money you need to make each month so you can feel good about all the work you have done. I always add at least $200. If I don't make $200 positive cash flow per month, it's just not worth the trouble. So in this case I would make the tenant buyers monthly payment $1,100/month. 700 + 100+ 100 = 900 + 200 (for profit) = $1,100 tenant buyer house payment.

$700/month	Your payment to the bank
$100/month	Insurance
$100/month	Taxes
$900/month	Money leaving your pocket
$900/month	Money needed to break even.
$200/month	Money to give me a positive cash flow.
$1,100/month	Payment required from the tenant buyer

Now, how much money do you want to make when you sell the house? I will go to realtor.com and see what houses like mine are listed for in my area. Let's say I determine that houses like mine, in my area are listed for $135,000 dollars. Now

I have a choice. I can stick with $135,000 as my asking price or not. It's my choice. There are several moving pieces that I put into my calculation. The tenant buyer will be in the house at least two years, maybe longer. What will the house be worth two years from now? How much will inflation increase the value of the house? I am taking all the risk here. It's my name on the bank promissory note. It's my name on the insurance policy. I have made it very easy for a family to move into this home and set up housekeeping immediately. What is that worth? In this example let's assume I set the RTO purchase price at $135,000.

For the first two years of the lease option agreement, I do something called an on-time credit. Each month that I receive a payment that is made on-time, I will reduce the balance owed by $300. The tenant buyer starts with a $135,000 purchase price. I receive a non-refundable option consideration fee of $5,000 before they move in. $135,000 − 5,000 = $130,000. Assuming every payment for the next 24 months is on-time, the tenant buyer will have a credit of $7,200 off the purchase price. 24 months × $300 = $7,200. At the end of two years, the perfect tenant buyer has paid the balance down to $122,800. Keep in mind you borrowed $115,000 and you have been making payments on that for two years. At the end of 24 months, you owe the bank $112,000. Now the spread between what you owe the bank and what the tenant buyer owes you is $10,800. $122,800 (what tenant buyer owes you) – $112,000 (what you owe the bank) = $10,800.

$135,000	Purchase price.
$5,000	Option Consideration.
$7,200	Payment On-time credits.
$122,800	Purchase price when the agreement expires.
$122,800	New purchase price at the end of 24 months.
$112,000	Balance you still owe to bank.
$10,800	This is your profit at the closing.

If you're a deep thinker, you're wondering, "How in the world can I possibly quit my day job doing one or two of these a year?" Good question.

If you look at the short term, not only did you make $10,800 at the closing, you made $5,000 when you received the option consideration and you made $4,800 monthly cash flow from two years of monthly payments. You really made $20,600. Does that make you feel any better?

$10,800	Profit when you sell.
$5,000	Option consideration.
$4,800	Positive cash flow. 24 months × $200 = $4,800
$20,600	Total profit

That's not the end of the story. Now let's think long term. So how are you going to quit the factory on $2,400 a year positive cash flow? $200/month positive cash flow times twelve months = $2,400. You must think bigger! What if you had ten RTOs going at the same time. 10 × $2,400 = $24,000/year. Don't forget, you have received $5,000 from each of these tenant buyers before they moved into your house. 10 × $5,000 = $50,000. You did the smart thing; you did not spend this $50,000. You did not increase your standard of living. You did not go on a Hawaiian vacation. You did not buy a brand new truck. You kept some of it as your business emergency fund and used the rest and began paying off your bank debt, one house at a time. Does this take time? Yes, but it's worth it.

What happens when you have paid off the mortgage on one of your RTO houses? Using the example in this chapter, your payment to the bank was $700/month. When the bank note is paid off, you are no longer making that payment. Therefore your monthly positive cash flow on this house just jumped from $200/month to $900/month. $900/month × 12 months = $10,800/year positive cash flow on just one property. Each time you pay off one of these mortgages, it's like shifting you real estate money making machine into a higher gear.

$0/month	Mortgage (you paid it off!)
$100/month	Insurance
$100/month	Taxes
$200/month	Cash coming out of your pocket
$1,100/month	Payment coming from tenant buyer
$200/month	Going out for taxes and insurance
$900/month	Positive cash flow per month

Don't stop now. Let's look ten years into the future. All 10 of your RTOs are paid off and your average positive cash flow on each house is $900/month. $900/month × 10 = $9,000/month positive cash flow. I'll bet you can survive on that!

$900/month	Positive cash flow from each RTO.
× 10 houses	RTO's that have no bank debt
$9,000/month	Total positive cash flow

When I quit the factory job I had 13 RTOs working and five of them were paid off. It was enough positive cash flow to equal my take home pay from the factory. That was the day I declared my FREEDOM from the factory. It had taken me ten years. This is not a get rich quick scheme. This is a way to gain financial independence and financial freedom so you can do what you want to do when you want to do it. No more asking permission if you want to go fishing tomorrow. You just get up in the morning and go.

As the economy began to improve and houses began to sell, I began to sell my RTOs. When a tenant buyer would move out, if I didn't want to own that house anymore, I would fix it one last time and then list it with a realtor and let it go. I took the profit from that sale and paid off the mortgage on one of my other RTOs. I continued buying houses and selling houses until all of my bank debt was paid off.

There's no secret to this process. You just need a burning desire to do more with your life than punch the clock. This is exactly how it works, and it is just that simple. However, you must be prepared for the curve balls and you WILL get your share of curve balls. Hang onto your profits.

10

Why Charge An Option Consideration

There are many reasons why I charge an option consideration. The main one is because that is what separates people who have a buyer's mentality from those who have a renter's mentality. Renters tend to be nomads. They believe they are only going to be there for a year or less before they move on. That's not who I want to do business with. I want to sell the house and I want to put someone in it who believes they want to buy it.

People who can come up with $5,000 cash have thought about home ownership. They want it. They believe it's possible. They don't spend every dime they make as fast as they make it. When these people give me $5,000 of their hard earned cash, they are less likely to leave. By turning over this amount of money, they feel like owners and are more likely to take care of the house.

I have charged less for the option consideration on smaller homes. I have had pretty good success with $4,000 for the 2 bed 1 bath homes. I always require the option consideration and the first month's house payment before I hand them the keys. So, even on the small homes, the amount of money they hand me before moving in, is very close to $5,000.

11

Why The
On-Time Credit

In every lease option agreement, I give buyers an opportunity to reduce the purchase price by $7,200 just by making their monthly payments on time. This is a very good motivator and it helps me determine early on if they are thinking as tenants or owners. If they think like an owner, they want to pay on time because they want to buy this house someday. If they think like a tenant, they don't care whether they pay on time or not because they never expect to own the home. It's one way to motivate the buyer to pay on time.

I have used higher amounts and lower

amounts for the on-time credit. I have found that $300 works best.

It says in the agreement that if the payment is one day late, they do not get the on-time credit. All payments are due on the first day of the month. If they mail their payment, the postmark must be before the first day of the month.

I have had RTO buyers call and apologize for being late and ask me what late fee they owe. I tell them there is no late fee; they simply do not get that month's on-time credit. They thank me and tell me they will do better.

12

Is There Really Any Call For Rent-To-Own Housing

Why would someone even consider doing a rent-to-own home? Is there really any call for rent-to-own housing? The answer is definitely "Yes," and let me tell you why. There are basically two ways to acquire a house to live in; you can rent a house or you can buy a house. There are not many choices outside of those two. You are offering a third choice: a rent-to-own plan. This plan offers several advantages that first time home buyers do not get.

They get to move in immediately. There is no

60 day or 90 day waiting period while you wait on appraisers, bank committees, inspectors, government paper shufflers, underwriters, etc. When you hand them the keys, they can start unloading their car.

Two years gives the tenant buyers time to clean up their credit, save a down payment, look for a good mortgage broker, and maybe even time for interest rates to go down.

Because I have given the tenant buyers two years to feel the responsibility of taking on all maintenance required on the property, they may decide home ownership is just not for them. Maybe they would rather go back home and live in mama's basement. At least they got to try it for themselves.

The tenant buyers get to live in the house before they buy it. It's a try-before-you-buy option. It's kind of like putting 5% down on a pair of shoes so you can wear them for a week to see if you really like the fit. If you don't like the shoes, you take them back. The shoe store gets to keep your 5% and you get to look for shoes someplace else. We all know that shoe stores don't do that, but I do. I let the buyers try the house on for size. They get to sleep in it. They cook in it. They have parties in it. They get to know the neighbors. They get to know the neighbor's dogs. Is it near a gun range? Is it on a busy street? Is it near the railroad tracks? Is it in a location where kids are cutting through your yard everyday going to school? The tenant buyers get to put these shoes on and try them out for a couple of years before they decide if they want to make it permanent.

These are all great experiences you have provided for the tenant buyers before they make the permanent decision to buy a home. You will have no problem finding candidates for your rent-to-own properties.

13

Handling The Phone Calls

The house is clean. There are no dead bugs anywhere. The windows are clean. You fixed all holes in walls and doors. There is fresh paint on every surface, ceilings, walls, doors, inside closets. Carpets are clean. There are no plumbing leaks. You placed rugs at the door for people to wipe their feet. Everything works. All doors open and close properly including exterior, interior, closet, and cabinet. All lights work and you put high lumen output bulbs in every fixture. You want the place bright. You have cleaned and/or painted the exterior of the house. If there was algae on the exterior, you bleached it off.

You have mowed the grass, pulled weeds, trimmed bushes and picked up all the trash and dead limbs. The fence, mailbox and gutters are straight. You cleaned out the gutters. The roof and gutters have been bleached clean. You have pressure washed the porch, straightened the fence, painted the shed. The TV antenna and all satellite dishes have been removed from the roof and yard. The place looks good and smells good, everything works and the neighbors love you.

You are ready!

You need a separate phone line to handle the hundreds of phone calls you are about to receive. I have an old-fashioned land line with multiple mailboxes. I program the phone so that when they call, it rings twice and then they hear, "You have reached the voicemail box of Jerry Hines. If you are calling about my rent-to-own home at 123 Maple street in Bedford, please press 1. If you are calling about my rent to own land on Hwy 42 in Carroll County, please press 2. If you have a house you wish to sell, please press 3. For all other matters please press 4 and leave a message."

The callers interested in my RTO house will press 1 and hear, "This beautiful 3 bedroom 1 bath house has a full unfinished basement, central heat and air. It comes with a stove, refrigerator, 0.5 acre fenced yard, and a 10 by 10 storage building. You are welcome to go out to the house ahead of time to walk around the yard and look in the windows. I will be showing this home at 6:00 p.m. on Thursday, June 12. I hope to see you there on June 12 at 6:00 p.m. You have a great day."

That's it. I don't tell them to leave me a message, because I don't want them to leave a message. I want them to show up for my party and often the showing looks like a party. I don't tell them how much per month or how much down; I don't give them any financial details. They will understand the plan better if they see my poster while I am explaining it. It really needs to be an eyeball-to-eyeball discussion. The truly interested people will make it to the showing. There will be people who want you to meet them some other time at their convenience. Don't do it. They won't show up. Tell them you will be showing the house every week until it's gone. They will have other opportunities. If it is truly important to them they will find a way to be there or they will send parents, spouse, adult children or someone to gather information for them. My first showing date is usually one week after I place the RTO signs.

Time to make some signs. You will have some wood scraps left over from your work on the house. Use these scraps to make yard signs. Approximately 3 feet wide and 1 foot high will do. I mount legs on the signs to get them at least a foot or more above ground level. I paint the wood white and the lettering black, red, or orange. Any color with good contrast on white will work. On the top half of the sign, I paint "Rent To Own." On the bottom half of the sign, I paint my office phone number "502-532-6084." In the middle of the sign, I paint an arrow that will point to the house. When my house is on the main drag through town I only put signs in the yard of the house. If the house is buried in a subdivision, I will put signs out on the main drag pointing to the house. The signs you place out on the edges of the subdivision will occasionally disappear. The signs in the yard of your house will almost never walk off.

Create and print 30 to 35 Home Ownership Applications. You're going to need them. (See the example in Chapter 15.)

Create a poster that will show how the math works on this deal. This will be a very important piece during your open house. (See the example in Chapter 14.)

The house is fixed. You have cleaned the house and yard. Your signs are ready.

Your voice mailbox is set up and ready to go. You have a briefcase full of lease applications. The poster is ready.

It's time to place the signs. Once you place the signs, don't hang out at the house. You will have people pull in and waste your whole day telling you all their sob stories and why you should let them move in with no down payment so they can destroy your home and disappear in the middle of the night, six months from today, when they are then two months late on their payments. Don't linger. Make everyone wait for the advertised showing day.

Go home and listen to your office phone ring off the hook. Don't be tempted to pick up. The first week after you put out your signs, it is not unusual to get 100 calls or more. 90% of these callers are people with no money and no desire to buy. They just want some new place to tear up. Wait and meet them all at the showing. You have something that all of them want and they see each other as competitors in a race to acquire your property.

I check my voice mail around 9:00 p.m. each

night. If someone did leave a message and asked me to call them back, I will return their call, but only one time. Do not return the calls with your cell phone. Use your business phone that is listed on the signs. Some people will call you day and night wanting special treatment. If they do not have a voice mailbox or if their mailbox is full, too bad. I do not chase them. If I do get a mailbox or they do pick up, I give them the financial details. When I tell them I am looking for someone who has $5,000 to use as a down payment, most of them tune me out. They are finished. You don't want people who see themselves as renters. You want people who think like owners. People who plan to be owners will have cash somewhere or have a plan on where to get it: 401K, Dad, Grandma, tax refund, etc. Stick with people who think like owners.

People will have the best stories. They have an insurance settlement coming soon and they will have the money then. Their great uncle just died and the money is hung up in probate but you will have it soon. A company bonus is coming soon and you will have it then. You're going to have to trust me on this one: if they can't hand you a stack of dead presidents before they move in, you need to find someone who can.

14

Getting Ready For The Showing

Create a poster. A good standard size poster is 22" × 28". The poster will have all the financial details of the deal. On the poster will be the purchase price, the expiration date of the agreement, the down payment, the monthly payment, and the amount of on-time credit you will allow. (See Exhibit A / The Poster).

When you see the numbers on my poster, don't forget, these are **rural Kentucky numbers.** Your poster will look exactly like mine except your numbers will be larger.

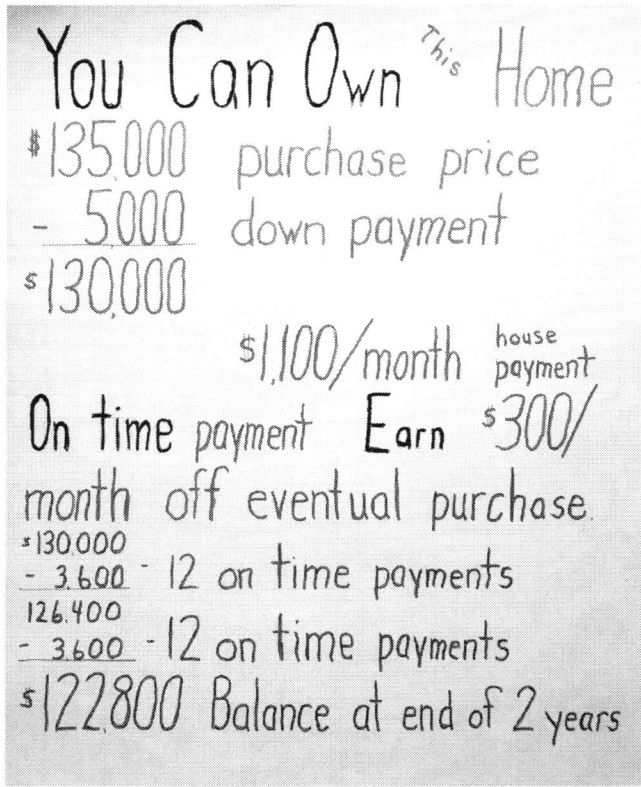

You have spent the week responding to phone call messages, picking up trash in the yard and checking on your pointer signs to find better spots for those that disappeared.

The day of the party has finally arrived.

Before you head to the party, make sure you pack these items:

1. 20 to 30 lease applications.
2. Half dozen ink pens.
3. Business cards.
4. The poster.
5. Your real estate logbook or whatever it is that you write your daily notes onto.

Relax! This is going to be fun! These people want what you have.

Be there at least 30 minutes early. I like to get there early enough to pick up dead bugs, open windows (during good weather), check the yard for trash, etc. I frequently have people sitting in the driveway waiting on me when I arrive 30 minutes early. Don't get stressed out. Introduce yourself. Open up the front door and tell them to go on in and look around while you get everything set up and the lights turned on.

Don't go dressed in a suit and tie or a fancy dress with high heels. Wear something nice but don't look like an executive. I wear a nice pair of black jeans and button up work shirt with my logo embroidered above the breast pocket. It looks professional but not fancy.

15

The Showing, It's A Party

The house is ready. The home ownership applications, ink pens, business cards and poster are spread out on the counter top in the kitchen. I always set up the kitchen as my home base. It's usually the best lit room in the house and it has counter space. I keep the applications in a stack close at hand because I want to hand them out. I don't want every tire kicker to waste my copy paper.

Show time.

People begin showing up. All the lights are on and the front and back doors are open. Your adrenaline is pumping, and you have a smile on your face because you know you are getting ready to come into some money.

I tell every family unit that comes into the house the same thing. I happily invite them in and then I tell them, "Look in every room, open every closet, open every cabinet, flush the commodes, whatever you want to do, then come back in the kitchen and I will tell you how the math works." Most will want to hear the math first because I am already standing in the kitchen and the giant poster with all the dollar signs has grabbed their attention. I'm good with that. I once had a house in Madison, Indiana where I had over 30 families come through the house in less than one hour. It was incredible fun. Some people are there out of curiosity. Some are looking for a place to rent, destroy and then move on. Young families with kids are there. Kids are running everywhere picking out their room. Young couples bring their parents to make sure I'm not someone who will take their money and not deliver on my promises. I've even had other investors show up to see what I'm doing.

When each customer is ready to see the math, I hold up the poster and start at the top. I explain all the numbers, top to bottom. At the end I ask if there are any questions. There are almost always some questions. The two that I get most frequently are, "Will you take less for the down payment?" and "Will you accept less for the monthly payments?" Now let me turn your attention to the Home Ownership Application. (See Exhibit B / Applicant Information Sheet on page 76.) I tell them if they are really interested in the home, pick up and complete the home ownership application. On that sheet they can tell me the largest down payment they can come up with and they can tell me the maximum monthly payment they can afford. I get to decide who I want in my house. Also attached to the home ownership application is the Applicant Information Sheet. (See Exhibit C / Home Ownership Application on page 77.)

JERRY HINES

Applicant (A)

Name:_____

Date of Birth:_____

S.S.No#:_____

Driver's License No.:_____

Home Phone:_____

Cell Phone:_____

E-mail:_____

Street Address:_____

City:_____State:_____Zip:_____

Applicant (B)

Name:_____

Date of Birth:_____

S.S.No#:_____

Driver's License No.:_____

Home Phone:_____

Cell Phone:_____

E-mail:_____

Street Address:_____

City:_____State:_____Zip:_____

Employment:

Employer's Name:_____

Employer's Address:_____

_____

Work Phone:_____

How Long on Present job:_____

Monthly Take Home Pay:$_____

Other monthly Income:$_____

Source:_____

By my signature below, I hereby give my
permission to investigate my credit and
employment history and I authorized release of
all credit related information.

Signature:_____

Date:_____

Employment:

Employer's Name:_____

Employer's Address:_____

_____

Work Phone:_____

How Long on Present job:_____

Monthly Take Home Pay:$_____

Other monthly Income:$_____

Source:_____

By my signature below, I hereby give my
permission to investigate my credit and
employment history and I authorize release of all
credit related information.

Signature: _____

Date: _____

Current Landlord: _____ Telephone: _____
How Long At Current Address? _____ Monthly Rent: _____
Reason for Leaving: _____
Previous Landlord (if less than 3 years): Name: _____

Telephone: _____ Previous Address: _____
How Long? _____ Monthly Rent: _____
Reason for Leaving: _____

List all occupants:
Name: _____Relationship: _____ Age: _____
Name: _____Relationship: _____ Age: _____
Name: _____Relationship: _____ Age: _____
Name: _____Relationship: _____ Age: _____
Name: _____Relationship: _____ Age: _____
Name: _____Relationship: _____ Age: _____

Home Ownership Application

Your Name _____Phone # _____

E-mail Address: _____

1. How much money do you have as a down payment? $_____

2. What is the maximum monthly payment you can afford? $_____

Please complete the information requested above and the Applicant Information Sheet attached and return them to Jerry Hines by one of the three following ways:

1. Scan and e-mail to **(Your email address)** (And call to make sure I received it.)
2. Regular mail to **Jerry Hines** at **(Your mailing address)**.
3. Bring completed application to the next showing of the home.

Thank you for your interest in this home.

Jerry Hines 502-532-6084

Make sure these people have a job and make sure you call their employer if they turn out to be your favorite home owner candidate. Be wary of those people who have been in their job less than six months. These people are nomads. If they can't hold a job, they are going to struggle to hold a house. If they don't have a job at all and are living on your tax dollars (i.e. the government sends them a check every month), let them go somewhere else with their money. If they won't work, they will never buy this house from you and that means they have the renter mentality. Occasionally, you will have people who won't completely fill out the applicant information sheet; they leave out vital information. They leave out just enough information that you will not be able to do a credit check or background check on them. These people have a criminal background they are trying to hide. Find someone else to put in your house.

Let's say you have a showing and hand out 12 home ownership applications. Several of the families filled out the application on the spot and gave them to you before they left. This doesn't happen every time but it does happen. I tell them that I do not make any decisions that night. I need time to review all applications and I will be calling their employers and references listed on their application. I tell each person I will call them back to let them know if they are chosen or not.

You've asked for $5000 down and $1000/month for this 3 bedroom 2 bath home.

The first applicant wrote that they can do $2000 down and $1200/month.

The second applicant says they can do $1500 down and $1500/month.

The third applicant wants to trade a 1979 Harley Davidson motorcycle for the down payment and wants to pay $750/month.

The fourth applicant has $30,000 to use as a down payment but he does not want his monthly payments to exceed $500.

Yes, This stuff really happens. You get to make the decision who you want to do business with for the next 2 to 20 years. Yeah, I know, my lease application says they only have 2 years to buy me out. We will get to that later when we review the lease option agreement.

That night you go home and pass out because of the adrenaline rush. Your voice is hoarse because you reviewed your poster over 20 times during the evening's festivities. The next day you pick who you believe is the best applicant and call their employer and landlord to verify the information given on the Applicant Information Sheet is accurate. I also go onto their Facebook page to see if they brag about how many times they got stoned last week or how many beer cans are stacked in their mom's basement or if they have slandered their current boss or landlord. I don't want to be in business with that person. It's my house and therefore my choice.

I have never accepted a motor cycle or truck etc. in trade for a down payment because what I always find is that what they want to trade is worth more as scrap metal than it is as a viable means of transportation. That has never worked out for me.

I like the people who have large sums of money to use as a down payment for two reasons.

1. The down payment is called "option consideration" and this money is non-refundable. Once they give me the option consideration, they don't get it back. Ever. It's mine.

2. When a person has a large sum of money invested in the rent to own, they are less likely to tear the house up and leave.

I favor people with large down payments as long as I can get a monthly payment that will cover all my expenses (PITI – principle, interest, taxes, and insurance) and still give me a little positive cash flow.

Occasionally you will have a nut case appear at your showing. At one particular showing, I had a house full of people, probably 10 or 12 families moving around. It was a circus. I was holding the poster up and describing the financial details to 15 or 20 people in the kitchen. One man, who had a real grouch going on, interrupted my speech and snapped at me, "What makes you think this house is worth $80,000 dollars? Have you had it appraised?" I took a breath and responded, "No, I have not had the home appraised. I own it and therefore I get to determine its worth." Then I looked back at the poster and continued with my math. There were no other challenges that evening. I had several Home Ownership Applications turned in at the end of the showing time. Just keep your cool and remember, you are the one with the power. You own the house. You call the shots.

16

Signing The Lease Option Agreement

You have picked your tenant buyer. They had the best application. You called their employer and everything checks out. You looked at their Facebook page to see if they are bragging about how many times they got stoned last week. They passed. You called them and they are meeting you at the house this evening with cash.

If there are two adults leasing this house, make sure they are both there.

They will want to give you the money as soon as they get there. Don't take it. Tell them you are going to read the lease option agreement to them line by line. (See Exhibit D / Lease Purchase Agreement on pages 85-91.) If they have any problem with the agreement, they walk away with their money and you keep the house. If the agreement is acceptable to all parties, everyone will sign the agreement.

Then I give them a copy of the Lease Option agreement and read it to them line by line. I take time to answer their questions. If they don't like the rules, you do not want them in your house. Your relationship with them will not go very well. Paragraphs 12 and 14 of the lease option agreement, Damage To Premises and Maintenance and Repairs, are probably my favorite paragraphs. After I read these paragraphs I look them in the eyes and tell them, "I'm not your mommy, your daddy or your landlord. I am your bank. You do not call me unless the place burns down or the roof blows off. Is that completely clear?" At this point, they look at me and nod. Now they know my expectations. It's a clear message and it works most of the time.

Lease with an Option to Purchase

This agreement is made and entered into on June 22, 2024 between Jerry Hines, herein referred to as Lessor, and John Wayne and Calamity Jane Wayne, herein referred to as Lessee. This lease is for a term of two years, to commence on July 1, 2024, and to end on June 30, 2026, at five o'clock p.m. The dwelling is located at 1200 High Noon Ave, in the City of Milton, County of Trimble, State of Kentucky.

1. **Lease Payment.** The Lessee agrees to make monthly payments in the sum of Eleven Hundred Dollars ($1,100) on or before the first day of each calendar month beginning June 1, 2024. The Lessor shall credit towards the purchase price at closing, the sum of Three Hundred Dollars ($300) from each monthly lease payment made prior to or on the due date. The Lessee will receive no credit at closing for any monthly payment that the Lessor receives after the due date specified in this agreement. A mailed payment must be postmarked **before** the due date to receive the credit.

2. **Form of Payment.** Lessee agrees to make the lease payment on time, each month in the form of cash, cashier's check or money order made out to Jerry Hines. The first payment must be made before moving in. All future payments will be mailed to Jerry Hines at (your home address) Kentucky, 40006.

3. **Option Consideration.** As consideration for this option to purchase, the Lessee shall pay the Lessor

a non-refundable option fee of <u>Five Thousand Dollars ($5,000)</u>. This amount shall be credited to the purchase price at closing when the Lessee timely exercises the option to purchase, provided the Lessee is not in default of this agreement. The Lessor will not credit this fee if the Lessee defaults in this agreement or fails to exercise the option to purchase. The form of payment must be cash, cashier's check or other certified funds made payable to Jerry Hines. The option payment must be made before moving in.

4. **Exclusivity of Option.** This Option to purchase is exclusive and non-assignable and exists solely for the benefit of the named parties above. Should the Lessee attempt to assign or transfer this option to purchase, this agreement shall be terminated.

5. **Closing and Settlement.** Lessee will arrange their own financing and agrees that closing costs in their entirety, including any points, fees and other charges required by the third party lender, shall be the sole responsibility of the Lessee.

6. **Default.** Failure to make the payment by the 10th of the month shall be considered default. On this date the Lessor may terminate this agreement by giving written notice of termination and begin the eviction process. When this lease is terminated, the Lessee shall lose entitlement to all lease credit and option consideration money. A violation of any part of this agreement will be considered breach of contract and this agreement will be terminated. For the Option to purchase portion

of this agreement to be enforceable and effective, the Lessee must comply with all terms and conditions of this agreement.

7. **Attorney Fees:** Violation of any of the conditions of this agreement shall be sufficient cause for eviction from said premises. Lessee agrees to pay all costs of such action or cost of collection of damages as a result of Lessee's breach of this agreement.

8. **Use of Premises.** The premises shall be used and occupied by Lessee exclusively. Lessee shall comply with all the sanitary laws, ordinances, rules, and orders of appropriate governmental authorities affecting the cleanliness, occupancy, and preservation of the premises, during the term of this agreement.

9. **Number Of Occupants:** ____Adults ____Children.

10. **Insurance.** Lessor has obtained insurance to cover fire damage to the building itself. Lessor's insurance does not cover Lessees possessions or Lessees negligence. Lessor is not responsible for and will not provide fire and casualty insurance for the Lessee's personal property. Lessee shall obtain an insurance policy to cover damage or loss of personal possessions, as well as losses resulting from their negligence.

11. **Alterations and Improvements.** Lessee shall make no structural alterations to the home without the prior written consent of Lessor. No walls shall be dismantled in any way. No roof penetrations permitted. All alterations, changes, and improvements

built, constructed, or placed on the premises by Lessee, with the exception of fixtures removable without damage to the premises and movable personal property, shall, be the property of Lessor and remain on the premises at the expiration or termination of this agreement.

12. **Damage to Premises. All** repairs are the responsibility of the Lessee.

13. **Utilities.** Lessee shall be responsible for arranging for and paying for all utility services required on the premises.

14. **Maintenance and Repair.** Lessee will, at his sole expense, keep and maintain the premises in good and sanitary condition and repair during the term of this agreement, this includes the plumbing, HV/AC and electrical fixtures. If for any reason the Lessor is required to pay for repairs or maintenance, this expense will be added to the purchase price of the home.

15. **Personal Injury and Property Damage.** Neither Lessor nor its principle shall be liable to Lessee, his family, employees or guests, for damage to person or property caused by Lessee or other persons, whether such persons be off the property of the Lessor or on the property with or without permission of Lessor; nor shall Lessor be liable for loss or damages resulting from failure, interruption or malfunction in the utilities provided to Lessee; nor shall Lessor be

liable for injuries elsewhere on the premises. Lessee has inspected the premises and binds himself to hold the Lessor harmless against any and all claims for damages arising from those who sustain injuries upon the leased premises during the term of this lease or any extension thereof.

16. **Destruction of Premises:** In the event the property is totally destroyed by fire, flood, earthquake or other act of God, this lease shall be considered terminated on the date of the event.

17. **Right of Inspection.** Lessor and his agents shall have the right at all reasonable times during the term of this agreement to enter the premises for the purpose of inspecting all buildings and improvements thereon.

18. **Surrender of Premises.** At the expiration of this lease agreement, the Lessee shall surrender the premises in as good state and condition as they were at the commencement of this agreement, reasonable use and wear thereof and damages by the elements accepted.

19. **Landscaping.** The Lessee may not cut down any trees without written approval from the Lessor.

20. **Abandonment.** If at any time during the term of this agreement, the Lessee abandons the premises, the Lessor may enter the premises by any means without being liable for any prosecution, and without becoming liable to Lessee for damages or for any payment of any kind. If Lessor's right of re-entry is exercised following

abandonment of the premises, the Lessor will consider any personal property belonging to Lessee and left on the premises to also have been abandoned, in which case Lessor will dispose of all such personal property and is hereby relieved of all liability for doing so.

21. **Environmental Disclosure.** Lessor has never tested the premises for radon gas, asbestos, lead based paint, mold or any other hazardous material and has no knowledge of its presence.

22. **Condition of Premises. Lessee has examined the premises, including the** grounds, all buildings and improvements, and agrees to accept the property in its "**as-is**" condition. Lessor makes no warranties or representations about the condition of the property.

23. **Application.** Any misrepresentations, misleading or false statements made on the application shall at the option of the Lessor, void this agreement.

24. **Savings Clause.** If any provision of this lease is determined to be in conflict with the law, thereby making said provision null and void, the nullity shall not affect the other provisions of this lease, which can be given effect without the void provision and to this end, the provisions of the lease are severable.

25. **Acknowledgements.** The parties have read this agreement and have asked any questions needed to understand its terms, consequences and binding effect and fully understand the contents of the agreement. There shall be no further additions or changes unless they are reduced to writing.

Purchase Option. It is agreed that the Lessee has the option to purchase real estate known as: <u>1200 High Noon Ave., Milton, Kentucky,</u> for the purchase price of <u>One Hundred Thirty Five Thousand Dollars ($ 135,000).</u> This option will remain in effect for the length of this contract only. Lessee will give Lessor 30 days written notice of their intention to exercise the option. If the option to buy has not been exercised by the expiration date of this agreement, this agreement is null and void. Entering into a new option to purchase agreement may be considered at the expiration of this agreement. At that time the agreement will have to be renegotiated. This purchase option shall not be effective should the lessee be in default under any terms of this agreement or upon any termination of this agreement.

The parties signing below have executed this agreement on the date noted below.

Lessor:		Date:	
Lessee:		Date:	
Lessee:		Date:	

At the end of the reading, you ask them if they have any questions. If everything is acceptable, you have them sign both copies of the agreement and you sign both copies of the agreement. You give them one and you keep one. They will lose theirs, but at least they started out with one. You need to keep your copy in a safe place. It will be very important in the future. They will give you the money. You will count the money and then you give them the keys. The Home is theirs. You're done. You drive off and they move in.

You have explained that tomorrow you will have the electricity and water shut off. It is their responsibility to get it transferred into their name. I remind them to get renter's insurance and why. It is now up to them to act like home owners.

Most of my meetings with the future lease option tenants go flawlessly; however, you will eventually have one that goes bad. I had one of these meetings where the married couple seemed OK at the showing. When they showed up for the reading and signing of the lease option agreement I got to see the dark side of the force. The wife was an angel. The husband was drunk. While I was reading the agreement, the husband acted like a spoiled ten year old child. He wandered in and out of the room while I was reading. He huffed and puffed like he had someplace better to be. He asked several questions leading me to believe that he did not want to do this. At one point I stopped reading and told the wife that maybe she should take her money back with her if her husband did not want to enter into this agreement. She told me she did want to do this and then she turned to this 230 pound drunk husband and told him to shut up. It was interesting to see. I was shocked. She turned to me and said, "Please continue." I began reading the agreement again, and at the end, she signed it and she told the 230 pound drunk to get over there and sign his name. I took her money and I gave her the keys. As soon as I pulled out of the driveway, I knew I had messed up. I should have politely asked them to leave. I should not have entered into this agreement with a drunk. It turns out, he was an alcoholic. He was in and out of court with DUI charges. He wore one of those attractive ankle bracelets that the court system loans people they call frequent flyers. She was usually late with the house payment but she did pay. Early in the lease, the drunk called me to the house to complain. He showed me the problem. I listened to his complaint then told him how to fix the problem that he created, then I left.

I think his wife straightened him out after I left. I never received any more calls after that incident. She finally kicked him out.

I tell you this story so you don't make the same mistake I did. When your future tenant buyer sets $5,800 cash on the kitchen counter and then acts like a jerk while you're reading the lease option agreement, tell them to pick up their money and leave. It's hard, but you will sleep much better at night if you do.

Regarding the Lease Option agreement that I use, yes, I know the book is titled Rent To Own but people don't understand lease with option to purchase. They do understand rent to own. Many of the people you will be talking with have purchased RTO furniture, RTO refrigerator, RTO big screen TV, RTO lawnmower, etc. The world understands RTO. Once you have reviewed the lease option agreement with them, they will understand it too.

I know there are people out there who watch Judge Judy on television and believe, they themselves are lawyers. They want to tell me that this lease option agreement is all wrong. Well, if I can get these TV lawyers to go back to the introduction of the book, they will see where I told them, "This book tells you one way to make money with real estate using the rent-to-own (RTO) philosophy. Notice I said one way. There are a thousand different ways to do it." I have had two attorneys read my lease option agreement. Neither of them found anything wrong with the document. In fact, one of the attorneys asked me if he could keep it and use it in his real estate business. I have been using this form for over 15 years and I have never had a problem with it, but I know you are going to write your own. That's Okay. Like I said, there are a thousand different ways to do it.

If you look on-line, you will find a hundred examples of lease option agreements to pick from. Develop your own. Create one that you can explain to a tenant buyer and make it happen.

17

What If Things Go Wrong

It's not a matter of IF things will go wrong. Things WILL go wrong. This is what separates the winners from the losers. Losers quit. They sell everything and are grateful they broke even. We, the can-do people, have written on the top of our goals list, "I WILL NOT QUIT." We would rather take a gunshot wound to the foot than work our day-job another year without hope. We've got to get out of this rut. Robert Kiyosaki calls it getting out of the "rat race."

The following is an experience that I have had more than once.

After the lease purchase buyers live in the house for 9 months, they just disappear. I mean they vanish. They have left behind a 40 cubic yard dumpster full of junk and they have done somewhere between $2000 and $5000 worth of damage to your house. You are mad as a wet hornet. You want to chase them down, bring them to court and squeeze their neck until money comes out of some body orifice. Don't bother. It's not worth your time. Clean the house up as fast as you can and do it again.

On a brighter note, one time I had a single man and his son doing an RTO with me in Madison, Indiana. He was on-time every month for 18 months. I never heard a peep. Then one month, no payment came. I called him several times. He never called me back. The thought that he may have died crossed my mind. I went to the house and knocked. No answer. I looked in the windows; all of his stuff was gone. I unlocked the door and went in. I mean, ALL of his stuff was gone and the place was swept clean. It was almost spotless. I had to fix two leaking faucets and I cleaned the windows. Two weeks later I was looking for someone else to give me $5000 down and $800/month.

I told you the second story so you know that I have more good stories than I do bad ones. But if you stay in this business long enough you to will have war-stories and WOW-stories.

Here is another good reason why you don't want to spend all your profits. I have written into my lease option agreements that "All repairs are the responsibility of the Lessee." However, I also have a sentence that says, "If for any reason the Lessor is required to pay for repairs or maintenance, this expense will be added to the purchase price of the home."

I received a call one evening in the middle of winter from one of my RTO buyers. The furnace has stopped working and they had no money. They needed my help. So, I called my HV/AC contractor and sent him to the house. Three days and $7,000 later, my RTO buyers had a brand new HV/AC unit. The purchase price they owed on the home just went from $83,400 to $90,400. I mailed them the paid receipt and an updated spreadsheet showing the new balance. They thanked me and life went on.

I will say it again. These horror stories are not normal, but they do happen. Your job is to be prepared both financially and mentally for bumps in the road to financial independence.

Philippians 4: 6–7

18

What Happens When The RTO Agreement Expires

The two years are up. The agreement is about to expire. You have heard nothing from the lessee about buying the home. Now what?

This is exactly what happens most of the time. Here is what I do. In the very beginning when I reviewed every sentence on the Lease/Purchase agreement with the tenant buyers, I told them (verbally) that if they needed more time before they were ready to purchase, I would allow them to stay in the house as long as they were not in default on any section of the Lease/Purchase agreement. I told them that their monthly payment would stay the same but their on-time monthly credit would drop from $300 per month to $100 per month.

I have several people who have been with me for over 10 years. I have no idea why they don't buy me out. With a principle pay down of only $100 per month they will be making payments to me for the rest of my life. That's not a bad thing. Let's say they only owe $40,000. $40,000 divided by $100 = 400. 400 months of payments = 33.3 years. Like I said, I don't know why they would choose to make payments to me for the rest of my life, but I don't mind.

19

Do I Ever Really Sell
An RTO Property?

Yes. I do sell RTO properties, but it is not very often. When I first got started doing RTOs, I only sold 2 in the first 10 years. There are many reasons for this revolving door of tenant buyers. Some have avoided taking on any responsibility their whole life. If the kitchen sink won't shut off or the front door doesn't latch properly or they got in an argument with the neighbor, rather than grow-up and fix the issue, they pack up everything and leave. These are the locusts. Some people simply never learned how to manage their money. They eat restaurant food 10 times a week. They max out every credit card buying clothes, video games and other stuff they do not NEED. They make huge car payments so they can impress the people they work with and the last bill to get paid is their house payment. These people almost always call it rent because in their mind, they know they will never own it.

The first RTO house I ever sold to a tenant buyer is a really good story. The tenant buyer called me one day and said he was ready to buy the home. He said, "I have the money and I want to give it to you today!" I told him I would schedule a closing with an attorney and he can give it to me then. "No," he said, "I want to give it to you today." Now when someone tells me they have $61,000 and they want to hand it to me today, that sounds pretty exciting to me. I want to relieve him of the burden of carrying that money around. He wanted me to meet him in the parking lot of a local bar at 9:00 p.m. that night. As I was thinking this through, I had a vision of me standing over a suitcase full of cash, in the dark parking lot of a bar, counting $100 bills. I felt a shiver run up my spine. I called the fellow back and told him, "Please don't bring cash. Please bring me a cashier's check." He laughed and told me he could do that. I did meet him in the parking lot. Yes, it was after dark. He handed me a cashier's check for $61,000 then he reached into his pocket, pulled out a wad of $100 bills, counted out 40 of them on the hood of my car and handed me $4,000 cash. We had been talking about another property I owned that had a shed in the back yard. He had inquired about the shed a week earlier and I told him I would sell the shed for $4000. Well, I guess he just bought the shed. I gave him a hand written receipt for the money. He went back into the bar and I drove home wondering, "Did what just happen, really happen?" The next day I drove to the bank to make a deposit and then to the attorney's office. I handed the attorney a note telling him how it all went down and that I wanted to transfer the deed into this fellow's name. Three weeks later the deed was put into the buyer's name. Weird stuff, but man is this fun!

20

Now I'm Making Money. What Should I Do With It?

First, keep good records. I use a very simple spreadsheet to track the payments received from my tenant buyer. (See Exhibit E / Payment Tracking Spreadsheet.) I keep track of every transaction. Every time my buyer makes a payment, I mail them a copy of the spreadsheet. I don't want any confusion about the money.

Date	Payment Type	Description
		Purchase Price of House
06/14/24	Cash	Option consideration
06/14/24	Cash	July payment
07/29/24	Money Order	August payment
08/27/24	Money Order	September payment
10/02/24	Money Order	October payment
11/07/24	Money Order	November payment
11/27/24	Money Order	December payment
01/01/25	Money Order	January payment
01/17/25		$1,500 HV/AC repairs (Lessor Paid)
01/28/25	Cashiers Check	February Payment
02/27/25	Money Order	March Payment
03/28/25	Cash	April Payment
04/27/25	Money Order	May Payment
05/31/25	Money Order	June Payment
06/30/25	Certified Check	July Payment
08/01/25	Money Order	August Payment
08/31/25	Bank Draft	September Payment
10/02/25	Cash	October Payment
11/06/25	Money Order	November Payment
11/11/25		$200 City Code Violation (Lessor Paid)
11/27/25	Cash	December Payment
12/10/25	Cash	Partial January payment
12/30/25	Cash	Final January payment

Amount Pd.	On Time?	Balance
		$135,000.00
$5,000.00	Yes	$130,000.00
$1,100.00	Yes	$129,700.00
$1,100.00	Yes	$129,400.00
$1,100.00	Yes	$129,100.00
$1,100.00	No	$129,100.00
$1,100.00	No	$129,100.00
$1,100.00	Yes	$128,800.00
$1,100.00	Yes	$128,500.00
		$130,000.00
$1,100.00	Yes	$129,700.00
$1,100.00	Yes	$129,400.00
$1,100.00	Yes	$129,100.00
$1,100.00	Yes	$128,800.00
$1,100.00	Yes	$128,500.00
$1,100.00	Yes	$128,200.00
$1,100.00	Yes	$127,900.00
$1,100.00	Yes	$127,600.00
$1,100.00	No	$127,600.00
$1,100.00	No	$127,600.00
		$127,800.00
$1,300.00	Yes	$127,300.00
$400.00		
$700.00	Yes	$127,000.00

Second, do not go buy a boat, jet ski, camper, new truck, or any other toy that depreciates in value. If you want to quit your job, you will put every dime of profit back into your real estate business. Use the profits as the down payment to buy more houses or pay down a mortgage to reduce the amount of interest you pay to the bank. I know it's hard for you to imagine but just think about that day when the bank loan on one of your RTOs has been paid down to a zero balance. No more mortgage payments on that house. What that does to your positive cash flow is truly amazing.

Keep some of that cash in a business checking account. You must be prepared for the curve balls, and you WILL get your share of curve balls. Hang on to your profits. I kept my factory job for 10 years while I was building my real estate business. Another reason to hang onto the profits is because of the taxes that will come due on April 15. Oh yeah, with your factory job, you used to get a tax refund from Uncle Sam each year. Those days are over.

21

Factory Flunkies Laughed At Me

Soon after I bought and sold the first house that I rehabbed and flipped, I bought business cards that said "I Buy Houses." I bought magnets for both sides of my car and the back that said "I Buy Houses" and listed my phone number. I hand painted 30 wooden signs that said the same thing, "I Buy Houses – 502-532-6084." I put these signs all over the three county area that I planned to do business in. It felt kind of funny because I really didn't know what I was doing yet. I really didn't believe I had the experience or knowledge I needed to say that my business was buying houses. It felt like a lie, but I wanted it to be the truth. I kept buying and reading real estate books and I kept looking for junk houses.

During this period of time I caught grief from co-workers, so-called friends and even some family members. There were difficult times at work because my minivan with over 200,000 miles sat in the parking lot with signs on it that said, "I Buy Houses." Yet, there I sat at my desk, 40 hours a week, just like all the other zombies coming in to punch the clock. I had several of the guys yell across the parking lot, "Hey! Did you buy any "HORSES" over the weekend?" and they laughed. It wasn't funny to me. It just made me mad and now that I can look back, that was a good thing. My anger made me even more determined that I would someday be able to walk into my supervisor's office and hand in my resignation and know that I would never have to ask permission to go for a dentist appointment. I would never again have to ask for permission to take a vacation. I would never again be told that I had to work a weekend or nightshift. The thought of being able to have that FREEDOM drove me to succeed.

Probably the scenario that will hurt the worst is when family members try to discourage you. That was the hardest one for me to deal with. My family had been programmed since the 1930s that the way to survive in this world was to get an education, then get a job at a factory with benefits and paid vacation time. It really is kind of sad how the factory setting has stolen the entrepreneurial spirit from Americans. Fortunately, my father-in-law was my greatest cheer leader. He had owned his own business since the 1970s and he loved what he did. When we talked, he always wanted to know what houses I had been looking at and what I had been learning from the books I was reading.

I kept plugging away at the house business. Every day I learned something new. I eventually bought an old, beat up pickup truck and put magnets on it. I made a lot more wooden signs. I learned that signs I stuck in the ground disappeared quickly, so I came up with a better plan. I would drive around early on Saturday mornings with a van full of handmade wooden signs. I would stop on the side of the road, pull a six foot step ladder out of my van, climb up the side of a telephone pole and nail the sign to the phone pole. Almost never did these signs disappear and yes, they did drive phone calls to my business phone.

I eventually bought a farm. The farm had a barn that sat on the side of a major highway. I had a 6'×12' banner made that said "I Buy Houses 502-532-6084." I mounted the banner to the side of the barn. The banner has paid for itself many times over.

In summary, don't let the negative, lazy, bored, fearful, whiners in your life stop you from realizing your dream of financial freedom! If I can do it, you can too!

22

Feel The Fear
and Do It Anyway

If you have not bought your first piece of investment real estate yet, what are you afraid of? Are you thinking about all the things that MIGHT go wrong? Are these thoughts paralyzing you? Stop that negative thinking! The stories you have read in this book are about things that have happened to me over the period of 18 years. They didn't all happen at once.

What if I can't sell it?

What if I can't find anyone with $5,000?

What if there are termites?

What if I get sued?

What if the tenant buyer trashes the house?

What if the tenant buyer has disappeared and stolen my appliances?

What if the neighbor complains to me about my tenant buyer?

What if my tenants quit paying me and they won't move out?

What if I run out of money?

What if high winds knock down a tree that damages my investment property?

Here is my suggestion; write down your every fear and below each fear, write an action plan. If the circumstance you fear most happens, what are you going to do about it? What's your plan? When you do this, you will find that every problem can be fixed. Every problem has a solution.

Regarding the "What If's" listed above, all of those challenges have happened to me in my real estate business. They didn't all happen at once. They happened over the period of 18 years.

The first time I had 10 RTOs going at the same time, the thought that occurred to me was, "What would I do if all my tenant buyers left at the same time?" This was crazy thinking. That never happened of course. But I did think about it. Even if it had happened, I had made up my mind that I was not going to quit. I was going to make this business work no matter what.

What if I can't sell it? *Do an RTO or rent it.*

What if I can't find anyone with $5,000? *Lower your option consideration or rent it.*

What if there are termites? *Pay an exterminator.*

What if I get sued? *Hire an attorney.*

What if the tenant buyer trashes the house? *Fix it and start over.*

What if the tenant buyer has disappeared and stolen my appliances? *Forget it and move on.*

What if the neighbor complains to me about my tenant buyer? *Go look the neighbor and your tenant in the eyes and take care of the problem.*

What if my tenants quit paying me and they won't move out? *Evict them.*

What if I run out of money? *Tighten your budget. Sell something. Borrow from your 401K.*

What if high winds knock down a tree that damages my investment property? *Call you insurance agent.*

Don't think of problems as problems; think of them as challenges. A challenge is something you deal with and learn from. A fellow that I greatly respect named Paul, once wrote, "God has not given us a spirit of fear and timidity, but of power, love and self-discipline." And in the words of the 19th century philosopher Friedrich Nietzsche, "What doesn't kill you makes you stronger." Now go out there and slay some dragons. You can do it!

23

Write Down Your Goals

I have a list I call my Frog-List. On that sheet of paper I have listed everything I want to do in the next seven days. Each day of the week displays a list of items I plan to do that day. Every evening before I go to bed I sit at the computer and update my list. I print it off, attach it to my clipboard and go to bed. When I get up the next morning, I know what I've planned to do and I go do it. If something is particularly scary or distasteful and I am prone to put this item off for another day, I put it at the top of the list and I do it first. I call this eating-the-live-frog. After I do this task that I dread, everything else on the list seems easy. That's how my daily to-do list got the name Frog-List. I eat the live frog first. A really good book to teach you how to manage your time better was written by Brian Tracy and is titled *Eat That Frog!: 21 Great Ways to Stop Procrastination and Get More Done in Less Time.*

That list of goals will only take you seven days into the future. The bigger question is, where do you want to be three months from now? Where do you want to be six months from now? How much money do you plan to make one year from now? Write it down. Once you get the next twelve months planned, it's time to dream big! Write down your goals for next year, for five years from now and for ten years from now. Don't sell yourself short. If you can dream it, you can do it.

Start today and write down a list of things you want to accomplish tomorrow.

At the beginning of every year, I rewrite my goals. Yes, they do change. That's okay. Some of the things I thought were important 20 years ago just don't seem that important now; other desires have taken their place.

There is a book by Dan Miller titled *48 Days To The Work You Love.* This book will give you some very helpful ideas on how to start setting goals. Another great book for instruction on how to set goals was written by Jack Canfield called *The Success Principles*.

My advice would be to keep your goals private. Don't tell anyone about your goals. Some people will make fun of you. Some people will flat out tell you that you can't do that. You will be ridiculed by the weak minded people who currently surround you. Family members and so-called friends will throw water on your fire of excitement and enthusiasm. Distance yourself from these negative attitudes. They can't see past their next paycheck but you can see ten years into the future. They can't understand you. You are tired of being mediocre. You want to excel in this life and they want you to stay miserable like them. Go find new friends. You could start by going to the meetings of your local real estate investors group. These people have goals similar to yours and their family laughed at them too.

If you want to be a millionaire, start hanging out with millionaires.

If you want a stronger marriage, start hanging out with couples that hold hands when they walk. Hang out with couples whose children behave. Hang out with couples who speak only positive words about their spouse.

If you want to grow spiritually, read your Bible more, pray more. Find a place where God is moving and join in the movement.

If you want to lose weight, hang out with skinny people and take note of their eating habits.

If you want to learn more, read more real estate books. Become self educated. I once heard that after you have read 100 books about a specific topic, you have then become an expert in that field. There is some truth in that.

Between the time I graduated from college until the time I felt compelled to self educate, I did not read one single book. Two decades wasted! Now, two decades after my enlightenment, I have a home library with over 400 books, tapes, and CDs covering topics from real estate, goal setting, time management, negotiating, estate planning, wealth building and more. I wasted two decades of my life; you don't have to.

Changing who you are takes work. It's hard, but it's worth it. Albert Einstein said, "Insanity is doing the same thing over and over again and expecting different results." If you don't want to be doing that same old dead end job when you're 70 years old, then act now. Do one thing today to propel you in the direction of your goals. I cannot make you change. Your spouse cannot make you change. Your mommy cannot make you change. You are the only one with the power to change you. I dare you to write your goals down today.

There is no shortage of money. Only a shortage of people with big goals.

24

Books That
Make You Rich

Owning a library with 50,000 books will not make you rich, but if you read them and actually do what they tell you to do, well.... try it for five years and find out for yourself.

These are books that helped me:

Are You Dumb Enough To Be Rich
G. William Barnett II
How To Be A Quick Turn Real Estate Millionaire
Ron LeGrand
Lease Purchase America
John Ross

Investing in Real Estate With Lease Options
Wendy Patton
Selling Houses With A Option To Purchase
Jay P. DeCima
How To Create Multiple Steams of Income
Peter Conti & David Finkel
Weekend Millionaire Secrets To Negotiating Real Estate
Roger Dawson & Mike Summey
Power Real Estate Negotiation
William Pivar & Richard Post
How To Find Hidden Real Estate Bargains
Robert Irwin
Make Money With Flippers, Fixers & Renovations
Gary W. Eldred
Secrets of a Millionaire Real Estate Investor
Robert Shemin
The Millionaire Real Estate Mindset
Russ Whitney
Start Small, Profit Big in Real Estate
Jay P. DeCima
Streetwise Investing In Rental Housing
H. Roger Neal
Multiple Streams of Income
Robert G. Allen
Acres of Diamonds
Russel H. Conwell

The Aladdin Factor
   Jack Canfield & Mark Victor Hansen
Before You Quit Your Job
   Robert Kiyosaki
Eat That Frog
   Brian Tracy
Total Money Makeover
   Dave Ramsey
Think and Grow Rich
   Napoleon Hill
The Psychology of Achievement
   Brian Tracy
The Millionaire Mind
   Thomas J. Stanley
When You See It, You'll Believe It
   Wayne Dyer
The Traveler's Gift
   Andy Andrews
The Success Principles
   Jack Canfield

You can find most of these books at thriftbooks. com for less than $10.00. If you read each book and apply the principles described, you will not have wasted one penny. You do not have to read all these books before you purchase your first investment property. I suggest you start with the first two on the list and then read one each month. After you have read the first two you will be motivated to go and buy your first investment property. After this, read one book each month to self educate and keep yourself excited about what your future is going to look like. If investing in real estate doesn't get you fired up, then you need to find something else that gets you excited about waking up in the morning. Life is too short to waste it doing the same old boring thing day after day. Go do something that makes you smile!

25

RTO Fix It Tricks

The toilet works, but the bowl looks terrible. You can't get the stain out of the bowl. No problem. Go to the hardware store and buy a gallon jug of muriatic acid. Sponge all the water out of the bowl. Fill the bowl to the stain line with muriatic acid. Cover the bowl with a towel or piece of plastic to hold the fumes in. Close the lid and let it sit for a couple of hours. Come back with nitrile gloves, a respirator, safety glasses and a toilet brush. Turn on the bathroom fan or open the window and scrub the toilet with the brush. You will be amazed. After 5 minutes of scrubbing, flush it down. Go ahead and flush 3 or 4 more times to make sure you have thoroughly diluted the muriatic acid in your plumbing.

If your house has a septic tank instead of city sewer, the process is a bit different. You start the same way by sponging all the water out of the bowl. In the case of a septic tank, pour a half inch or so of muriatic acid into the bottom of your mop bucket. Stick your toilet scrub brush into the bucket and then move the acid filled brush to the toilet and begin scrubbing. This process takes a few minutes longer, but it works just as well. You do it this way for a septic tank because you don't want that much muriatic acid going into your septic system all at one time. There is a chance that a large slug of acid could harm the good bacteria in your tank.

Your countertop has a large burn spot on it where someone had moved a hot pan straight from the stove to the Formica. It's ugly. Now what? You don't need to replace the entire countertop. Try this: Cut out the bad spot of the counter top and install a cutting board in the hole. It works and it looks good. YouTube is your friend!

The shingle roof has black streaks and algae growing on it. Buy a car wash brush, the one that comes on a five foot pole. The brush has fairly long bristles and it is soft. Mix 50% bleach and 50% water in a bucket. Take the bucket and carwash brush on the roof. Start at the top and work your way down. It's not perfect but it's pretty close. Don't use a pressure washer or a hard bristle brush, this will remove a protective layer from your shingles and cause premature aging of the roof.

You've put three coats of white primer on the walls and there is still a spot that keeps showing through the paint. Buy an aerosol can of oil base white spray primer. I like the Zinzer white spray primer best. I spray this on the spot and come back two hours later to see if I can find the spot. Rarely does this spot require more than two or three passes with the Zinzer spray primer.

You just bought a small house, 2 bedroom, 1 bath. The tiny kitchen has an ugly, broken dishwasher taking up space under the counter top. I'm sure that the tenant buyers will not take care of the dishwasher and it will have a very short life span. So, I remove it. I measure the hole and find an under the counter cabinet that will fit in that hole. I either paint it or stain it to match the rest of the cabinets. Done. The cabinet will last much longer than the dishwasher. The tenant buyers can wash their dishes by hand. It is possible, you know.

Everything in the house you just bought is covered in dog hair. This is normal. In your negotiations, you asked for, and received, the stove and refrigerator.

Surprisingly, both work. If you want to extend the life of the refrigerator by several years, get someone to help you tip the refrigerator back so the bottom is exposed. Vacuum all the dog hair off the coil on the underside of the fridge. There will be a thick mat of hair clinging to the coils. When you get this hair cleaned off, the fridge will thank you. Stand it back up and enjoy several more years of operation.

There are trees in your yard, tall enough that you will have leaves clogging the gutters this fall. Go ahead and cough up the money for metal gutter leaf guards. You have already cleaned out the gutters but the tenant buyer will never do that. The gutters will clog again. The rain will go over the gutters, soak through the foundation and into the crawl space or basement. You don't want that. It will take you four hours to install these metal guards. You will never drive by that house again and see trees growing out of the gutters like they were when you bought the house.

26

Retirement Party

When I turned in my resignation at the steel mill, my boss said he wanted to throw me a retirement party. I told him I wasn't retiring, I was simply going into business for myself. Besides that, I was only 56 years old. He wouldn't take no for an answer. So, on my last day he bought 20 pizzas and threw a retirement party for me. It was fun, but I would have been just as happy to have slipped out quietly and disappeared.

At the retirement party, no one at the steel mill was making fun of my "I Buy Houses" signs anymore. A couple of people asked me, "How did you do it?" What they really wanted to know was, how did I break free from the factory rat race and gain financial freedom? What was the secret? It was no secret. I told them that for the past 10 years I have been working 40 hours per week for the factory and another 30 hours a week building my real estate business. Every day for 10 years, when I would leave the factory, I would go to one of my rehab houses and work there for another 3 to 4 hours. 8 a.m. to 4 p.m. at the factory and then 5 p.m. to 9 p.m. working toward financial freedom. I also put in 8 to 12 hours on most Saturdays. No more television, a lot less time riding my ATV and a lot less time hunting. I did make some sacrifices but after 10 years, my wealth building machine was producing a positive cash flow equal to the take home pay of my rat race job. Was it a little scary to quit getting that bimonthly bump to the checking account? Yeah, you bet! But what a glorious day it was, that very next Monday, when everyone I knew was going back to the factory to punch the clock, and I knew, I would never have to do that again. I would never again be told when I could or could not take my vacation. I would never again have to ask permission to go to the dentist. The freedom I felt seeing the factory gate in my rear-view mirror for the last time was indescribable!

At the retirement party a 74 year old co-worker

asked me, "What are you going to do with all that free time?" I told him, "Anything I want!" He walked away with a confused look on his face. I couldn't imagine still working there when I was 74 years old and he couldn't imagine life without working there. How sad!

27

The Legacy

Now that I have been buying and selling real estate for 18 years I can look back and see some unexpected great things that have occurred.

When I bought my first investment property, I had one child in college, one in high school, one in Middle school and one in elementary school. Because my family had a front row seat to watch my life change during my struggle to make it in real estate, some amazing things have happened in my family's life.

All of my children got to see firsthand how to build equity in a house with hard work and the sweat of your brow. They got to see that even if a house is ugly today, almost everything is fixable. One can buy an ugly house that no one else wants, put time, money and labor into the house and create a product that is very desirable. The three who were still living at home when I began my business became paid laborers and got hands-on experience in several of my cleanouts.

All of my children are adults now. Each of them bought houses that needed work and acquired them at a good price. All of them have fixed up their properties and have very nice homes now.

My goal now is to keep encouraging this entrepreneurial spirit in the people around me. I encourage my family. I encourage the people at church that come to me asking for advice regarding real estate. I want the next generation to experience financial freedom sooner than I did.

Successful people WANT you to succeed! Why is that? Because it's fun! The look on a person's face when they achieve their goals is a beautiful thing. It's fun to hear the excitement in a person's voice when they tell you about the changes that are occurring in their life! This is fun stuff.

What will you do to make a positive impact on future generations of your family? They're watching you!

28

Stories With Happy Endings

There are a lot of people around you who will try and crush your dreams. They will try to discourage you from achieving your goals. They don't want you to succeed; they want you to stay stuck in the same rut they are in. They will tell you stories of lazy realtors, bankers that make you feel like a beggar, unscrupulous lawyers, and of course destructive tenants. Yes, those people exist, but for every poor example, there are good people who will want to help you succeed. Your quest is to find those good ones.

Spend less time listening to the naysayers and

more time listening to people who have been helpful to you. As you grow your business, you will meet good dependable people. When you do, ask them about other good people. Your electrician may know a good plumber. Your realtor may know a good attorney. Good people attract good people. As you buy more and more properties you will find the professionals that will make doing business fun.

In a seminar some years ago, Ron LeGrand was talking about the professionals who you are going to work with when buying and selling houses. His advice was to assemble your dream team with professionals that are people you would enjoy having lunch with. Why would you hire someone that you do not enjoy being around? I took his advice. It makes this business fun.

GOOD REALTOR STORY

I had been driving around looking at houses to determine if I wanted to make offers on any of them. This exercise generated many questions, so I drove to my realtor's office to see if I could get some answers. While I was in his office, he asked me if I had seen a certain house. It was a three-bedroom, one-bath brick home on a half-acre lot that sat on the side of a hill. I knew the house, but I had only been in it once, probably five years earlier. He told me he had been speaking with the owner. This house needed a lot of work. Would I be interested? I told him that I am always interested. He did not give me any financial details. He told me to go look at it; the side door was unlocked. So, I went to the house. Wow, it was a mess. The yard looked like a jungle. It was hard to see the house from the road because of all the vegetation. Trash was everywhere, a forty cubic yard dumpster full of trash to be exact. And then I saw the reason no one wanted this house. The entire front of the house was falling off. The foundation had shifted and pulled all the brick off the front. At the front door, I could put my entire arm between the bricks and the wall studs. It was bad. This was going to be a serious foundation rebuild. I stood on the front deck that had slid about six inches downhill away from the house. I looked up at the porch roof and it too was sagging to match the porch displacement. Now that I knew the seriousness of the situation, I drove back to the realtor's office. When I came in, he asked me what I thought. I told him I probably wasn't the buyer he was looking for. It was more than I had ever tackled. He told me to make an offer. I told him that I don't enjoy making offers that will make the sellers mad. If the seller is mad, it takes some of the fun out of it for me. He asked me again to make an offer. After squirming in the chair for a couple of seconds I told him that the half acre of jungle with water and electricity was maybe worth $8,000 but I still wasn't sure I wanted to take on a project of that magnitude. He smiled, leaned back in his chair, and said, "Would you give $5,000 for that property?" Well, I was shocked, but I could see that he was serious. As soon as the shock wore off, I said, "Yes." He picked up the phone and called the seller. He asked the seller if he could put him on speaker phone and told him the buyer was in the room. The seller agreed. Five minutes later I was filling out the purchase agreement to buy a three-bedroom one bath brick house on a half-acre of ground for $5,000. And that's not the end of the story. Four weeks after the closing, I had picked up all the junk in and around the house. It did fill a 40 cubic yard dumpster, clear to the top. I had trimmed all the trees, mowed the waist high weeds, battled bumble bees and wasps, and ripped out junk fencing. The house looked good from the road. I was almost ready to begin the reconstruction process when the same realtor came driving up the driveway. He looked around and was impressed with what he saw. We stood in the driveway talking and he asked me if I would be interested in selling the house just as it is, right now. My answer was, "Sure, what are you thinking?" He asked me how much money I had invested in it so far. I did a quick calculation of my expenses. He came up with a number he believed it would sell for in its current condition. I drove back to his office and filled out the listing agreement. Four weeks later, I sold that house and made $10,000 profit! I never even touched the foundation! All I did was make the place look good from the road.

GOOD INVESTOR STORY

The second house I ever bought was at a USDA foreclosure auction. It was early January, and it was cold. The auction was held inside the house. The temperature inside the house was around 15 degrees. Besides the USDA representative, only three of us showed up to bid. As the USDA representative read the rules of the auction, I studied my competition. I knew one of the fellows. He was a long-time entrepreneur and successful local investor who I knew would be able to easily out bid me. I did not know the other man. When the rules had been read, the USDA man announced the starting dollar amount and asked for someone to start the bidding. There was silence for a few seconds then the seasoned investor, gave the first bid. The third man made a bid and then I made a bid. After that, the local investor never bid again. It was back and forth between me and the third man. I eventually won the bid. When it was finished, the local investor walked over, shook my hand and congratulated me. He told me it was a good house and that I would do well with it. I thanked him and he walked out while I stayed to sign the paperwork. The investor could have easily out bid me on that house, but he let me have it. I really appreciated that, and I never forgot it. And that's not the end of the story.

About ten years later I had my son-in-law with me. We were standing at yet another USDA auction. The weather was much nicer this time. After walking all around the house, I struck up a conversation with the only other bidder to show up for the auction. I asked what they would do if they bought the house. She pointed across the street and said, "I live over there and I was hoping to buy this house so my daughter and her family could live closer to me." Wow, family is very important to me too. I like it that my brother lives across the street. My parents live about a mile away and my grown children all live within an hours drive. I thought about the good times I have with family because they live so close. While the USDA representative was reading the rules of the auction, I decided what I was going to do. When the representative asked for the beginning bid, I pointed to the lady and said, "You make the first bid." She made a bid $1 more than the required amount stated by the USDA representative. I looked at him and said, "I do not want the house. The lady has the winning bid." I walked over to her, shook her hand, and said, "Congratulations on the winning bid, it is a good house." She looked astonished. She thanked me and I left. My son-in-law and I had a great conversation on the way home about how much fun it is to be able to return a blessing, after being on the receiving end.

GOOD BANKER STORY

It was early in my investment career. This was before I began the RTO business model. I was new to buying, fixing, and selling houses. My job at the factory had been eliminated. I was living on severance money and unemployment. I had three houses going and I had run out of cash. One of the houses was listed with a realtor but the other two were still in need of repairs. I had gone to several banks to ask for money to get me over the hump so I could finish work on the other two houses. With no J.O.B., no bank would help me. I couldn't blame them. It did look a little weird. I was asking a bank to loan me money when I could show no income. I only had experience flipping two houses at that time. The last bank I tried was very small, only one location, no branches. I made an appointment and met with the bank President. I showed him my information and told him everything. He listened and then kindly said, "Jerry, I want to loan you the money. I know you would work yourself to death to repay it, but I could never get the board of directors to approve the loan when you have no income. If you would just go down the street to McDonald's and get a job, I will get you the money you need." He wanted me to succeed. I never forgot that moment. I still do most of my business through that little bank. It's fun to do business with them. They always have time for me when I walk in. In case you are wondering, I did get the money to finish the other two houses, but not from a bank. A relative was asking me how the house flipping business was going and I told him the story. He asked me how much money I needed to finish the houses. I told him $30,000 would do it. He gave me a check that evening for $30,000. I won't forget that either. It got me over the hump. When I sold the houses, I paid him back. I am surrounded by good people, and so are you!

GOOD ATTORNEY STORY

Let me tell you a story about "The Snake House." Yes, there was a house in my county that had sat vacant for years. It was known as the Snake House. The legend was that the house was full of snakes and no one wanted a house full of snakes, except me, of course. I found out that two sisters, in their 60's, had inherited the house. They didn't want it, but neither did anyone else. I contacted them and worked out what I thought was a pretty good deal. Both sisters signed my one page purchase agreement. The attorney completed the title search and all the documents were ready to sign. We were at the closing. One of the sisters was calm and reasonable. The other sister was negative and angry that she wasn't getting more money for the house. The more this negative, angry sister talked, the madder I got. I kept my mouth shut, but it was hard. I let the attorney do his job. Lucky for me, this attorney was good at his job. The angry sister was informed that she was going to have to pay two hundred dollars in closing costs and she flipped her wig. She said she was not going to sign anything. She was going to walk out. By this time, I had heard enough of this woman's mouth and I was ready to put my cashier's check back in my pocket and head back to the bank. She can keep the "Snake House," I thought. Well, the attorney kept his cool and somehow convinced her that the money she was going to pay in closing costs was really going to come out of my pocket. I had become so angry with this woman that I lost focus on the explanation that the attorney gave her, but she must have been satisfied because she accepted his explanation and I became the proud owner of the snake house. For those of you who like to hear the end of the story, here it is. I cleaned out the entire house, attic to basement. There were no snakes in the house. I did not even find a snake skin in the house. I cleared $30,000 when I sold this house. Not bad for a house that no one wanted.

29

Grandpa, Are You Rich?

One day I had the privilege of being the substitute home school teacher for three of my grandchildren. After an hour or so we began the math lesson. It wasn't too long before I could tell there was a concept that my seven year old grandson just couldn't grasp. I tried every way I could think of to describe this process on paper. He just didn't get it. Finally I went into another room and pulled out an envelope containing approximately 200 one dollar bills. I thought maybe this hands-on visual would make the lights come on.

We worked for probably another 45 minutes

trying to grasp this one concept. It didn't work. By this time the other two grandchildren had become involved in the money madness and there were one dollars bills scattered all over the kitchen table. As we gathered up the bills, my grandson asked me, "Grandpa are you rich?" I thought for just a moment and responded, "Yes, Finn. I am rich. I have a healthy body. I have a family who loves me and I have a savior, Jesus Christ, who died for me so that I can have eternal life in heaven. Yes, Finn. I am rich."

There is nothing wrong with working hard in this life and becoming the best you that you can be. There is nothing wrong with having a lot of money. But if your only measure of success is your net worth on a financial statement, you will have missed out on the joy, peace and love that could have been yours all along life's journey.

I heard these words spoken at a seminar a few years ago, "I am a spiritual being here on this planet having a human experience." What are you going to do with your human experience? How will you use your life to enhance the lives of those you come into contact with everyday? If you chase after wealth for no other reason than to have money, you will have missed the joy and peace that God wants all of his children to experience. Myles Munroe said "The greatest tragedy is not death, but life without purpose." Who are you? Who does God want you to be? What does God want you to do?

1 Corinthians 10:31

1 Peter 4:11

Isaiah 43:7

Romans 11:36

About the Author

 JERRY HINES began investing in real estate in 2006, while still working at the factory. He worked in both chemical recycling and steel manufacturing facilities. Between 2006 and 2016, he worked 40 hours a week at the factory and evenings, weekends and holidays, growing his real estate business. In 2016 Jerry happily quit "work" to pursue the career he loves; buying and selling real estate. Jerry's financial success was achieved purchasing almost all of his investment real estate within a 30 minute drive of his home.

Jerry has been married to the same beautiful "patient" woman for 40 years. He has been blessed with four children and nine grandchildren. Now celebrating eight years of freedom from the factory, he says, "Life just doesn't get much better than this!"

Ecclesiastes 3:22
"So I saw that there is nothing better for people than to be happy in their work."

Made in the USA
Columbia, SC
03 February 2025

53197367R00087